What to do when Gluten-Free

TMGF

PRODUCTIONS

For permission requests, e-mail to the contact, addressed "Attention: Permissions Coordinator," at the address below.

Ordering Information:
info@tmgfproductions.com

We are not doctors, physicians or dietitians.
Always consult with them for guidance and information. The symptons of celiac disease are numerous and may vary depending on the severity of your condition.

Printed in the United States of America.

ISBN 978-0-9971311-1-6

Winiford Publishing
Amarillo, Texas 79109

To my parents,
Pat & Nancy.

The day before didn't seem so...
Is gluten-free the way I should go?
The doc said I have celiac sprue.
Oh me! Oh my! What do I do?!

But like he said, I will wait.
Celia Ann will aid me in this fate.
And just like that at 10 o'clock,
The front door pounded with a knock-knock-knock!

I opened the door & what do I see...
A lady & a dog staring at me.
With a blink of an eye she barged in right,
Introducing herself & Glu-tyn-o-mite!

I'm here to help you with your lifestyle diet.
It may seem hard until you try it!
Come now, let's start with your kitchen first,
that's where gluten is the worst!

We must be thorough & safe from cross-contamination,
So clean these counters & any other cooking station.
Oh this pantry, it's tainted terribly bad!
Glu-tyn-o-mite come! This gluten must be had.

Toss the can-opener, toaster & baking supplies!
Anything with breading or malt say your goodbyes.
This wheat! And rye! And bulgar too!
Hydrolzyed protein we are getting rid of you!

Wait! Please not those cookies, graham crackers or rolls...
Why the marinades, broth & charcoals!?
"Oh my dear," Celia Ann replied, "look closer & you'll see,
Always look at all the ingredients, gluten is sneaky."

There's wheat starch that acts as a binder.
And when contaminated it doesn't act any kinder.
It hits you hard; you're down for the count.
Now let's move on to something you may discount!

Caramel Color*

Modified Wheat Starch

Maltodextrin*

Vegetable gums

*May be derived from Wheat

She asked, "Read that box. What does it say!?"
I exclaimed, "It says wheat free! Hip hip hooray!"
"Oh no!" She said, "That will set your tummy aflame!
Wheat free & Gluten-free are not one in the same."

"Oh, Celia Ann what will I eat!?
Is it really that bad if I cheat?"
She replied, "Oh my dear, don't be a fool!
Gluten-free is your golden rule!"

I hereby decree a gluten-free lifestyle for life.

But it's not that bad, you'll find your groove,
Once you learn what to remove!
It's not about what you can't eat, but what you can.
Let's hit the store, I've got a game plan!

And don't you worry you soon will eat!
For Celia Ann will cook you a tasty treat!

Tara A. Murray

Tara was diagnosed with celiac disease in 2008.
She asked the doctor, "So instead of four bowls of cereal a day, just one?".
Sadly no, she could have nothing that contains gluten, such as
wheat, rye or barley. So what's left!? A whole new gluten-free world!
Through her celiac journey, Tara started TMGF Productions,
"A New Way to do Gluten-Free".

She also consults and speaks as a gluten-free expert.
She wants all to know, "It's not about what you can't eat,
but what you CAN eat!"
Tara is the author and illustrator of a "Gluten Free Series".
Visit www.tmgfproductions.com for more information.
Tara resides in Amarillo, Texas with her husband.

CAN YOU FIND SOME OF THE ITEMS THAT NEED TO BE THROWN OUT AND STARTED FRESH?

BROTH   CAN-OPENER   CHARCOAL   COLANDER
CONDIMENTS   CUTTING BOARD   JAM   JELLY
MARINADES   SAUCES   SEASONING   SIFTER   SPONGE

```
C U T T I N G B O A R D
H C O L M E D R T S M C
A S A U C E S O S P A O
R M S L U R E T Q O R L
C H T J B S O H W N I A
O S E A S O N I N G N N
A R R M L L N E S E A D
L C A N O P E N E R D E
J E L L Y A S I F T E R
A C O N D I M E N T S R
```

Answer Key:

```
C U T T I N G B O A R D
H C O L M E D R T S M C
A S A U C E S O S P A O
R M S L U R E T Q O R L
C H T J B S O H W N I A
O S E A S O N I N G N N
A R R M L L N E S E A D
L C A N O P E N E R D E
J E L L Y A S I F T E R
A C O N D I M E N T S R
```

For more word search activities
and games, visit
www.tmgfproductions.com

TMGF PRODUCTIONS

TMGF Productions is a new way to do gluten-free.
So what does that mean?
We offer informational & interactive materials for
children with celiac disease or a gluten-free lifestyle.
We know that going gluten-free is a lifestyle change,
& at times it's hard!
But with a little help from TMGF, gluten-free will be
as easy as 1, 2, 3 ...!

WINIFORD

publishing